MARCHING THROUGH THE FLAME

The Children of Selma Marched Through the Flame and Did Not Burn: A Civil Rights Memoir

by

Chief Henry E. Allen

DORRANCE
PUBLISHING CO
EST. 1920
PITTSBURGH, PENNSYLVANIA 15238

Dorrance Publishing Co
585 Alpha Drive
Suite 103
Pittsburgh, PA 15238
Visit our website at *www.dorrancebookstore.com*

ISBN: 978-1-4809-2596-0
eISBN 978-1-4809-2182-5

Dedication

To the students from R. B. Hudson high school,

In the years from 1963 to 1965, who would face the many dangerous challenges that we accepted. We were called "freedom fighters," putting our lives on the line without fear.

Charles Bonner, Terry Shaw, Cleo Hobbs, and Charles Mauldin—they were the leaders in the Civil Rights Movement who came face-to-face with Sheriff Jim Clark, who arrested every student he could and put them in jail.

Thanks to Lewis Marshall who carried the American flag and Bobby Simmons who let the world know we planned to vote. Giving thanks to our young freedom fighters: JoAnne Blackmon, Lynda Lowery, Sheyann Webb, Rachel West Nelson, Mary 1. Allen, and D. C. Allen.

Thanks to all who gave so much to the Civil Rights Movement. We marched through the flame and did not burn! May God forever bless you.

Contents

I

I'm from East Selma

I was born on December 30, 1944, in a small three-room shotgun house, no inside bathroom and outside running water. Food was cooked in a wood burning stove, an icebox with no electric power. My mother would buy a twenty-five cent block of ice three times per week.

My father, Henry E. Allen, was unable to read or write. He had an alcohol problem. He would spend all his earnings on whiskey. He was a poor provider for his family. My mother, Ethel Lee Allen, could read and write. She had to stop school in the fifth grade. Her mother had a massive stroke.

My mother got married at the age of fifteen. There were four boys and one girl and my grandmother. A family of eight members lived in that house. My father took a job with a pipeline out of Tampa, Florida. My father came back to Selma and moved my mother and the three youngest, two brothers and one sister, to Tampa, Florida. They left me and my oldest brother with my grandmother at the age of eight years old. My grandmother taught me how to cook and houseclean.

A year later, my mother and the rest of the family moved back to Selma because my father had started a second family in Tampa, Florida. My mother was torn apart. My grandmother was the family leader. She kept the family together.

Her religious faith was Catholic. So I was also of the Catholic faith. I also attended Catholic school in the third grade. My mother and father were Baptist.

On December 24, 1959, my grandmother passed away. That was the darkest day in my life. When she died, the family fell apart. There were days we did not have food to eat. I sold drink bottles, scrap metal, and cans to earn fifty cents. This was a day's work to earn fifty cents. We were very poor and living in poverty. I never wore shoes the right size; they were either too small or too big. The shoes were always hand-me-down shoes. To keep pants from falling down, we used a strip of cloth to hold up our pants. When your shoes and tennis shoes would fall apart, we used wire to hold them together.

Christmas at my house was a very sad day. We had to make our own toys. We never owned a bicycle. My cousin worked for the drugstore, riding a bicycle. When he came to visit, I learned to ride a bicycle on the drugstore bicycle in order to buy schoolbooks and clothing.

I had to work the cotton field, the cornfield, pick tomatoes, cucumbers, and peas to earn money to buy all my school needs. I would register for school in September and work the fields until the last of November. Then I would return to school.

The school that I attended was a two-story building: two rooms downstairs and two rooms upstairs. There were forty to fifty children in these classrooms. No cafeteria, all outside restrooms. This school only went to the third grade. When you passed to the fourth grade, you had to go on the other side of town to complete the fourth grade to the sixth grade.

If you lived in East Selma, people looked down on you. Growing up for me was very hard. At the age of nine years old, I found my first job, working at a café one block from my house. My job was taking out the trash, and helping to wash dishes.

I lived in a community where both blacks and whites lived. At the age of ten, I started a new job next to where I lived. Mrs. Mary Pepper owned a community grocery store, and her son owned a television repair shop in the back of the store. His name was Luther Pepper. They were whites living in a mixed community. Mrs. Pepper loved all the people; she was a pillar of the community. Mrs. Pepper always made sure that I had food to eat. I even had enough food to take home for the whole family.

The Lord placed me in the care of Mr. and Mrs. Pepper to provide for me. Mr. Pepper was a father-like figure to me. He provided all my needs through elementary school. Mr. Pepper bought my first pair of eyeglasses for me in the fifth grade and took care all of my high school needs.

My father died December 7, 1962, at the age of sixty-two years old. My mother is now eighty-seven years old. My brother D. C. Allen was killed in a car accident on December 20, 1965, the same year as Bloody Sunday and the passage of the Voting Rights Act. My sister died in the Bronx, New York, in 1983 of cancer. They both were Civil Rights foot soldiers. They were on the Bridge on Bloody Sunday. They were also in the march to the State Capital in Montgomery.

Even in the midst of segregation and Jim Crow, the good Lord placed me in the care of a white family in the early sixties. They loved me, and I loved them. Mr. and Mrs. Mary Pepper have passed on. I still communicate with the family.

While working for Mr. Pepper, I learned so many different skills: installing television antenna towers, repairing televisions and radios. I was truly blessed to get a jump start in my life early. I enjoyed what I was doing and loved going to school. Mr. Pepper put me in charge of all the installations that had to be done. That made me very proud of myself. I was earning ten dollars per week.

I always tried to do my best. In the ninth grade and tenth grade, I had perfect attendance. I had to walk from one side of the town to school. When I was in the eleventh grade attending R. B. Hudson High School, Mr. Pepper hired a white kid from the A.G. Parrish High School. At that time there was an all-black school and an all-white school.

The white kid's name was Porter. Porter and I would often discuss school homework. Porter and I had a hard time trying to understand why the both of us were in the eleventh grade and I was studying books two years behind him. The both of us agreed that something wrong was going on.

I worked very hard so that my name would be listed on the honor roll. On my last progress report I had missed the honor roll by one point. On my new progress report, I had a B+ average. When I received my new progress report, my name was not on the honor roll. I went to my English teacher and asked her, "How could I have possibly made a C- in her class? My average was a B+ in her class."

She looked at me and said, "You are from East Selma, and in my eyes you will never rise above a C- student." What my English teacher said to me made me hurt all over.

I began to cry. I went into the boys' restroom. I said, "Lord, what must I do? I cannot go on like this."

Proverbs 21:1, "The king's heart is in the hand of the LORD, Like the rivers of water; He turns it wherever He wishes."

I was a very poor kid and needed all the help that I could get. Mr. Pepper hired Mr. Dewey Mitchell from Union Springs, Alabama, to repair television record players and radios. Mr. Mitchell and his wife became second parents for me.

Most of my young life was spent around white males. Craig Air Force Base was a pilot training center where the Air Force pilot learned to fly jet airplanes. Many of the jet pilots worked part-time for Mr. Pepper. The pilots spent a lot of their time helping me with my homework and teaching some things about life.

At this early stage of my life, the Lord was shaping and molding me for the task he had planned for my life journey. God gave me the courage to continue on. At this stage in my life, I would place my head on my desk and talk to the Lord.

Typical Shotgun House

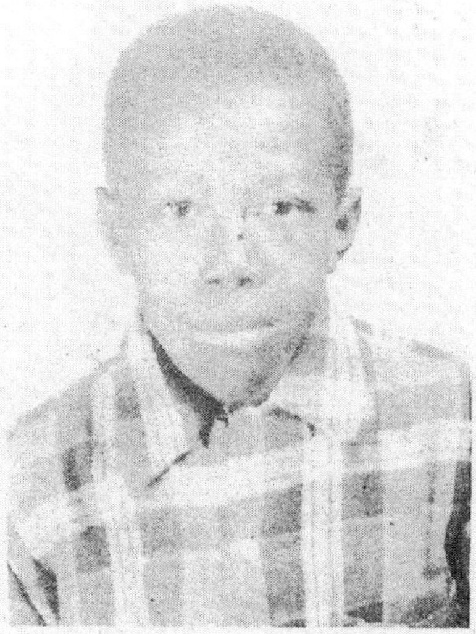

Author Henry E. Allen

The First Two-room Schoolhouse

Brother D.C. Allen

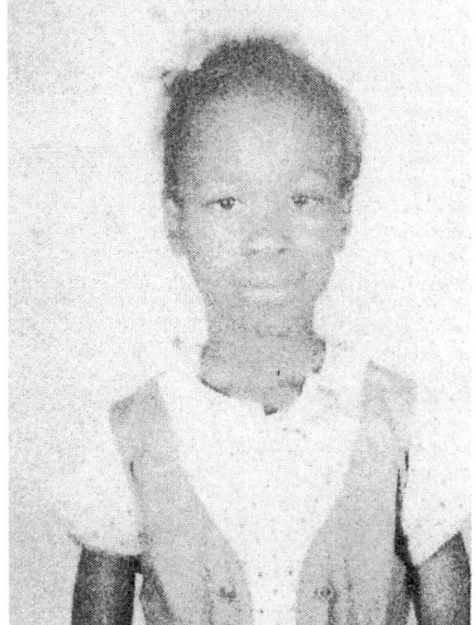

Sister Mary L. Allen

II

We Lead the Movement in Selma 1963-1965

The Civil Rights Movement began in Selma, Alabama, in the year of 1963. I was a junior in R. B. Hudson High School in the eleventh grade.

R.B. Hudson High School was the starting point for student involvement at the beginning of the Civil Rights movement in May, 1963.

R.B. Hudson School was named after a black educator, minister and businessman, Richard Byron Hudson. The school was erected in 1949.

Richard Byron Hudson was born in Uniontown, Alabama, and was a graduate of the Alabama Colored Baptist Normal and Theological School (now Selma University). He served as principal of Clark School for forty-one years; during his tenure, the enrollment increased from less than one hundred students to one thousand three hundred students. He was president of the Alabama State Teachers Association, secretary of the Alabama Baptist Convention (1897–1931), and secretary of the National Baptist Convention (1903–1931). He also served as the Sunday School superintendent of Tabernacle Baptist Church for thirty years.

R. B. Hudson was a Selma businessman, proprietor of a coal business and a dominant figure in Selma's black community. It was fitting that in 1949 the newly erected black high school bore his name. The school educated students in grades 7–12 and remained R. B. Hudson High School until a Federal court ordered it renamed in 1970 and made it a junior high school as part of the plan to hasten integration. In later years, the National Park Service has declared the R. B. Hudson High School as part of the Historic National Trail.

In the summer of 1963, R. B. Hudson High students played a major role in the beginning of the Civil Rights Movement in Selma, Alabama. The torch was lit by students in the 11th grade. This movement was started by Bernard Lafayette and his wife, Colia, who were members of the Student Nonviolent Coordinating Committee (SNCC). Bernard Lafayette taught and trained some students from R. B. Hudson High School to be leaders in the Civil Rights Movement in Selma, Alabama. Their major role was to teach blacks in Selma how to fill out applications to register and vote.

Students from R. B. Hudson High School were taught in the basement at Tabernacle Baptist Church by Lafayette and his wife, Colia. The first trained students that would take applications through the community were Charles Bonner, Bettie Fikes, Evelyn Mann, Cleo Hobbs, and Terry Shaw.

This was Lafayette's first class. There were many nights the students would stay overnight in the basement of Tabernacle, learning how to do sit-in demonstrations and when you should fall and cover up.

Bernard Lafayette brought fear to this old cotton port city of Selma, Alabama, the seat of Dallas County. The black community was in fear.

One teacher had the courage to let Bernard Lafayette live in her household. Mrs. Margaret Moore was the only one in Selma who would allow Bernard Lafayette and his wife to live in her house without fear. We, the students, loved her.

Teachers who encouraged the R. B. Hudson High Student freedom fighters included Ms. Loretta Carter, who gave us love and support, and Mr. Perry Anderson, who worked with Mrs. Moore and Ms. Carter.

All the black pastors were afraid to let Bernard Lafayette hold a mass meeting in their church. Rev. L. L. Anderson asked his Deacon Board for permission to hold a mass meeting in the church basement. Out of fear the Deacons said no to Rev. L. L. Anderson.

In return he called them "a bunch of cowards" and shamed them. Out of shame, the Deacons said yes, we could hold our very first mass meeting at the Tabernacle Baptist Church on Broad Street and Mintor Avenue in the fall of 1963. Four of my classmates were team leaders. The reason for the mass meeting was the right to vote. Since 1901, the county and the state of Alabama had a system to deny you the right to vote if you were black.

In the midsummer of 1963, Bernard Lafayette was beaten very badly by a Klansmen on the same night Medgar Evers was killed in Mississippi, trying very hard to keep blacks from voting.
Lafayette left Selma on September of 1963 for Birmingham to check on his wife, who had left Selma to help the Birmingham Civil Rights Movement.

Public Safety Commissioner Eugene Bull Conner had gave the firefighters the order to open fire hoses on the demonstrators, who were students, and on Lafayette's now-pregnant wife. For a long period of time, Selma had no one from SNCC to lead the movement.

After Bernard Lafayette left Selma, going to Birmingham, student Charles Bonner called the SNCC office in Alanta, Georgia, asking for help.

While we were waiting, the church bombing happened at the Sixteenth Street Baptist Church in Birmingham, Alabama, on Sunday Morning in 1963. Four young girls were killed.

In support of the Birmingham protestors, Charles Bonner led a student Voting Rights Drive march to the Selma Dallas County Courthouse in protest of how blacks were treated by Sheriff Jim Clark. This was the first march in Selma!

On that day students were escorted to the City Jail and booked for marching without a permit. Sheriff Clark had in mind that, by placing the youth in jail, this would stop them from protesting and marching.

A torch had been lit that no man could put out. This was just the beginning of all that the students of R. B. Hudson High School would do for the Civil Rights Movement. From 1963 to 1965, more than three thousand students led by those from R. B. Hudson High School were placed in jails in Selma and neighboring counties.

In 1964, Sheriff Jim Clark was so frustrated and angry at his inability to control the students that he prompted Governor George Wallace to order mounted state troopers to Selma.

The troopers, along with Sheriff Jim Clark and his deputies, attempted to remove every African American from the streets, running them down until they found shelter.

Terry Shaw would take the lead in the downtown drug stores and eating places. SNCC organizers arrived in Selma to help stage the sit-in demonstrations. Their names were Prathia Hall and Worth Long.

In the sit-in demonstrations, students were hit, pushed, knocked down, and placed in the city jail for trying to sit at Whites Only locations.

At the City Jail, Worth Long was beaten very badly and got death threats. He never stopped his work trying to change the course of segregation and helping us students to be strong in the Voter Registration Drives.

We, the students, were told that we should stop the sit-in demonstrations and working to get people registered to vote. The students' main goal was to protest and march for the right to vote.

SNCC Chairman John Lewis led three hundred students to protest, and all protestors were arrested, including John Lewis.

County Sheriff Jim Clark and his deputies harassed people waiting in line and attacked SNCC workers. County Sheriff Jim Clark began to push and hit blacks as they waited in line to register.

Only two days per month were blacks allowed to try to register to vote. On October 7, 1963, author James Baldwin and his brother David and Comedian Dick Gregory and his wife Lillian were arrested for picketing with the students on the registration day.

This became known as Freedom Day. All the applications were turned down except five.

The Dallas County Voters League had a registration drive to get people out and register.

Mr. Ernest Leon Doyle served as the first vice president of the Dallas County Voters League.

Mr. Doyle was a very special person in my life: a man of great wisdom, quick minded, fair, honest, slow to anger.

He was my mentor and an icon to me and the community. He served in the United States Army in World War II. He was a foot soldier in the Civil Rights Movement.

Mr. Doyle's civil rights activities began in the early 1950s. On January 23, 1963, Mr. Doyle and seven other courageous persons were called the Courageous Eight.

They formed the Dallas County Voters League (DCVL) and began the monumental task of empowering blacks to exercise their right to vote.

In July 1964, Dallas County Circuit Judge James Hare issued an injunction barring black people from meeting in groups of three or more to discuss civil rights.

The intention was to stop groups marching to challenge the Public Accommodation Act and attempting to register to vote.

Rev. F. D. Reese, who taught for the Selma City School System and pastored two churches, said, "But the eight of us kept meeting, trying to figure out how to revive the movement."

In addition to Doyle and Reese, there were Marie Foster, a widow working in the dental office of her brother; J. D. Hunter, an agent for a black insurance company and minister; the Rev. Henry Shannon, Jr., a barber and minister; also Mrs. Amelia Boynton, who owned an insurance agency; Ulysses Blackmon, a teacher at the Lutheran Church School; and James Gildersleeve, a principal at Lutheran Church School.

At that time there were thirty-five thousand black residents. Only eighty-six blacks were registered as voters in the city because of the literacy test black residents had to pass to qualify to register.

Mr. Doyle was also a politician and public figure. He served as one of the first black city councilman since the Reconstruction era.

He took office in August, 1972. He also served as Dallas County president of the NAACP. In December, 1964, Mr. Doyle and the Dallas County Voters League invited Dr. Martin Luther King to Selma, Alabama, to lead the voters registration drive.

Now Reverend L. L. Anderson and the Tabernacle Baptist Church became a main target for Sheriff Jim Clark and his deputies.

Dr. Martin Luther King was arrested and placed in the city jail. When Mr. Ernest Leon Doyle was also arrested, they shared the same jail cell. They were bailed out of jail by the Southern Christian Leadership Council.

Dr. Martin Luther King and Mr. Ernest Leon Doyle were the planners for the March 21, 1965, Historic March from Selma to Montgomery, the second successful March following Bloody Sunday. Mr. Ernest Leon Doyle carried a large white banner proclaiming the Selma NAACP.

In all, his work laid the foundation for all African Americans, including all the Selma youth from age six and above for their voting rights in the United States.

Mr. Ernest Leon Doyle departed this life on October 25, 2011. My true friend, a father figure and my icon. Father, I stretch my hands to thee.

Teenage girls that gave so much help and time to the Civil Rights Movement included Bettie Mae Fikes and her singing of the civil rights songs. Nobody could do it like Bettie. I enjoyed stinging with her. She was the leader of the choir: "We shall overcome some day."

There were other teenage girls in the choir: Evelyn Mann, Carolyn Doyle King, my sister Mary Allen, Carry Manuel, Johnnie Mae Holliman, Mary Melton and many more young girls.

As a student I had very little fear. We told Jim Clark that we were ready to go to jail.

We had the Civil Rights Act of 1964 signed by President Lyndon B. Johnson.

We caught on fire fighting for our civil rights. We went and integrated white soda fountains in all our drugstores.

We had a drive in what we called "Thirsty Boy."

Some of our students were hit with billy clubs. We didn't stop going to jail. We kept marching.

Governor George C Wallace gave state trooper commanders full authority to do all that they could to stop the marching.

Jim Clark and Al Lingo ran over students with their horses, and they tried to kill me.

I ran for my life. An elderly lady opened her door to save my life from Al Lingo's state troopers on horseback.

We had a wave of demonstrations. Our plan was to fill up the city and county jails in all surrounding counties. Our plans were carried out. The students had done all that we could do. We had made the grownups look shameful.

The teachers at R. B. Hudson High decided they would march to the Dallas County Courthouse and register to vote.

Reverend F. D. Reese, president of the Dallas County Voters League, had a very tight schedule. He would help the student freedom fighters when time allowed him. He led the teachers march from Clark School to the Dallas County Courthouse for the right to vote. He was confronted by Sheriff Jim Clark, who pushed Rev. Reese with a billy club in a very ugly manner.

The teachers left the courthouse with a lot of courage. We, the students, were very happy. We no longer felt we were alone.

The school superintendent came to visit our school, R. B. Hudson High, and asked the principal "if he could control those nigger students." The superintendent was very angry at the principal because most of his seniors were leading the marches and demonstrations. The principal did not say a word to the superintendent.

We called the principal a coward, not knowing what a black man had to put up with in a society ruled by white males.

At first the principal did not try to stop the students from leaving the school. Then in the hallway leading to the school main entrance and exit, the school superintendent tried to block the main school exit door.

We moved him aside and exited the school into the parking lot, and we went to Brown Chapel Church for more marching.

We picketed segregated stores and demonstrated at the courthouse for the right to vote.

The superintendent told the principal that any senior missing any more days from school for civil rights marches would not graduate.

When the principal shared that message with all the seniors, it sent shock waves through the whole senior class.

We as seniors had a big decision to make. We were told by the principal and teachers not to miss any more days from classes. We could march after school was over. We kept on marching for freedom and the right to vote.

Reverend Joseph Ellwanger was the president of The Birmingham Council on Human Relations, which provided behind-the-scenes support for civil rights work. In 1963, he was president of the Alabama Lutheran Academy in Selma.

On Saturday, March 6, 1965, Ellwanger organized a march in Selma, Alabama, to support voting rights. He and 72 white Alabamans who wanted to openly support voting rights marched to the courthouse steps in Selma, where they were confronted by hostile whites singing "Dixie."

They came and left without any violence that day, and Ellwanger himself returned to march in Selma on "Turnaround Tuesday."

Saint Michael's Edmundites had run a mission in Selma since 1937 that served underprivileged African Americans in the South.

Father Maurice Ouellet, pastor of St. Elizabeth's Church, risked his life by preaching for social justice and supporting the efforts of the Civil Rights Movement in Selma.

Dr. Martin Luther King and the Southern Christian Leadership Committee arrived in Selma to help out with the voter registration drive.

Sheriff Jim Clark did not know what to do. Before the march to the Edmund Pettus Bridge, Dr. Martin Luther King had to leave for Atlanta. More than three thousand demonstrators had been arrested and placed in jails in the county and outside the county.

We were now getting ready for a very dangerous march. We knew that trouble lay ahead. Children were asked not to get on the front line.

This was the very first time grownups took the lead, children in the rear.

On March 7, 1965, more than five hundred marchers gathered at Brown Chapel AME Church in Selma, led by Hosea Williams and John Lewis.

Jim Clark, the Sheriff of Dallas County, and Public Safety Director Al Lingo mounted on horseback. The marchers were ordered to disperse. Major John Cloud of the State Troopers ordered the Troopers to move in on the marchers.

The news media were there and sent pictures across the nation.

Sheriff Jim Clark, Al Lingo and mounted troopers whipped and rode horses over every marcher they could hurt. It did not stop at the Bridge. It went on and on throughout the night.

Students walked through the flame on Bloody Sunday! Charles Mauldin took his position on the front line with John Lewis and Hosea Williams.

It took courage to get on the front line. We knew that something was going to happen, but what? Charles was just a teenage student and showed no fear that Sunday.

No marcher expected to be beaten with billy clubs, sprayed with tear gas, and run over with horses.

Marchers were lying on the ground, unable to get up. Many were taken to Good Samaritan Hospital for treatment.

Sheriff Jim Clark and the state troopers did not stop at the Edmond Pettus Bridge; they chased marchers all the way back to Brown Chapel Church.

The State Troopers on horseback continued trying to hurt marchers. When they got close to you, they had cow prods to shock you with. This went on all night long.

This was the first March on March 7, 1965.

The second March was led by Dr. Martin Luther King. Federal Judge Frank Johnson made a ruling blocking the marchers from marching. Dr. King went against Judge Johnson's ruling and led a march to the Bridge, stopped, kneeled and prayed, and returned back to Brown Chapel.

The third March was held on March 17, 1965. Judge Johnson handed down his decision approving the SCLC's proposal to March from Selma to Montgomery.

The final March was held on March 21, 1965, leaving Brown Chapel Church to the state capital in Montgomery, Alabama.

On March 25, 1965, the marchers arrived at the State Capital to meet with Governor George C Wallace. He refused to come out and talk to Dr. Martin Luther King. Freedom is not free. Jimmy Lee Jackson lost his life for freedom. Reverend James Reeb lost his life for freedom. Rednecks at the white

Silver Moon Café hit him with a billy club on the head. Viola Liuzzo lost her life fighting for freedom, killed by Klansmen. Jonathan Daniels, seminary student fighting for freedom, lost his life in Hayneville, Alabama, helping people get registered to vote.

We enjoy the freedom—the right to vote—because these four brave soldiers gave their all so others could live!

We are the forgotten children who caused the Voting Rights Act to be passed by President Lyndon B. Johnson, who signed the Act on August 6, 1965.

Challenging Words From Rev. Martin Luther King, Jr.

"Nonviolence is the answer to the crucial political and moral questions of our time: the need for man to overcome oppression and violence without resorting to oppression and violence. Man must evolve for all human conflict a method which rejects revenge, aggression and retaliation. The foundation of such a method is love."

"Faith is taking the first step even when you don't see the whole staircase."

"A man who won't die for something is not fit to live."

"I have a dream that one day on the red hills of Georgia, the sons of former slaves and the sons of former slave owners will be able to sit together at the table of brotherhood."

Selma and Dallas County Jail

Young Student Protestor

Rev. Joseph Ellwanger

Tabernacle Baptist Church

Register
Now
SNCC

One Man
One Vote
Register
Now

John Lewis, leader of the Student Nonviolent Coordinating Committee, is attacked by a state trooper during the attempted march on the state capitol,

Lawson State Community College

Bessemer Campus

R. B. Hudson High School

Father Maurice Ouellet

Historic Brown Chapel Church

Jimmy Lee Jackson

Jonathan Daniels

Viola Liuzzo

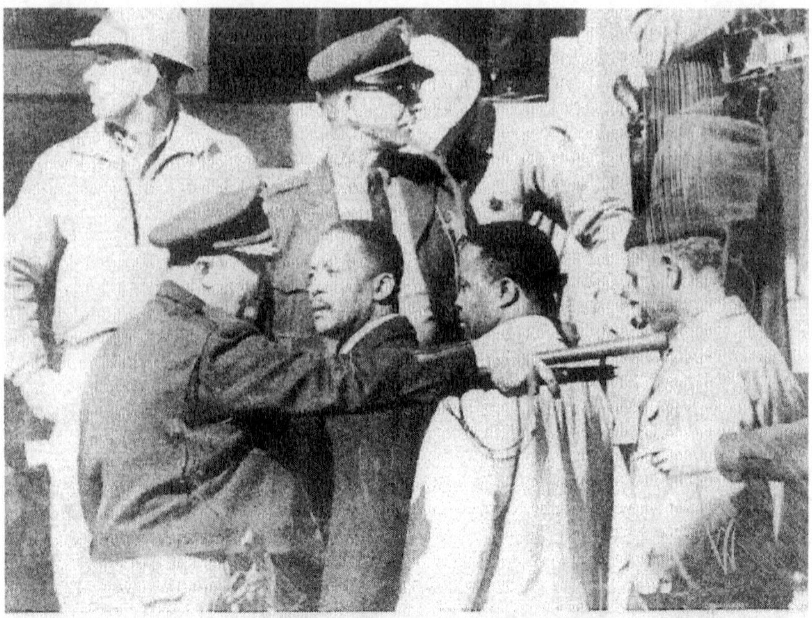

Dallas County Sheriff James Clark orders African American voting demonstrators to leave the Dallas County Courthouse in Selma on January 19, 1965.

John Lewis and Hosea Williams

Rev. James Reeb

Marchers on the Edmund Pettus Bridge during the Selma to Montgomery march in 1965.

Montgomery, Alaba

Rev. Frederick Reese, Courageous Eight (Courtesy of the National Voting Rights Museum and Institute)

[illegible] Blackmon, Courageous Fight (Courtesy of the National Voting Rights Museum and Institute)

Bernard LaFayette Jr. at the National Voting Rights Museum in Selma, standing in front of two photographs from 1963: one a mug shot from his arrest, the other from when he was attacked in Selma

VOTING RIGHTS ACT

August 6, 1965

Rev. H. Shannon,
Courageous Eight (Courtesy of the National Voting Rights Museum and Institute)

Back to the Beginning!
With Bernard Lafayette Again

March 7th, 1965 - Marching to the Edmond Pettus Bridge, Bloody Sunday

Mayor Joe T. Smitherman with
Congressman John Lewis

All Students – the First to March – on the Way to Jail

The Historical
R. B. Hudson High School

Challenging Words From Rev. Martin Luther King, Jr.

"Nonviolence is the answer to the crucial political and moral questions of our time: the need for man to overcome oppression and violence without resorting to oppression and violence. Man must evolve for all human conflict a method which rejects revenge, aggression and retaliation. The foundation of such a method is love."

"Faith is taking the first step even when you don't see the whole staircase. "

"A man who won't die for something is not fit to live."

"I have a dream that one day on the red hills of Georgia, the sons of former slaves and the sons of former slave owners will be able to sit together at the table of brotherhood."

Rev. J. D. Hunter, Courageous Eight (Courtesy of the National Voting Rights Museum and Institute)

James E. Gildersleeve, Courageous Eight (Courtesy of the National Voting Rights Museum and Institute)

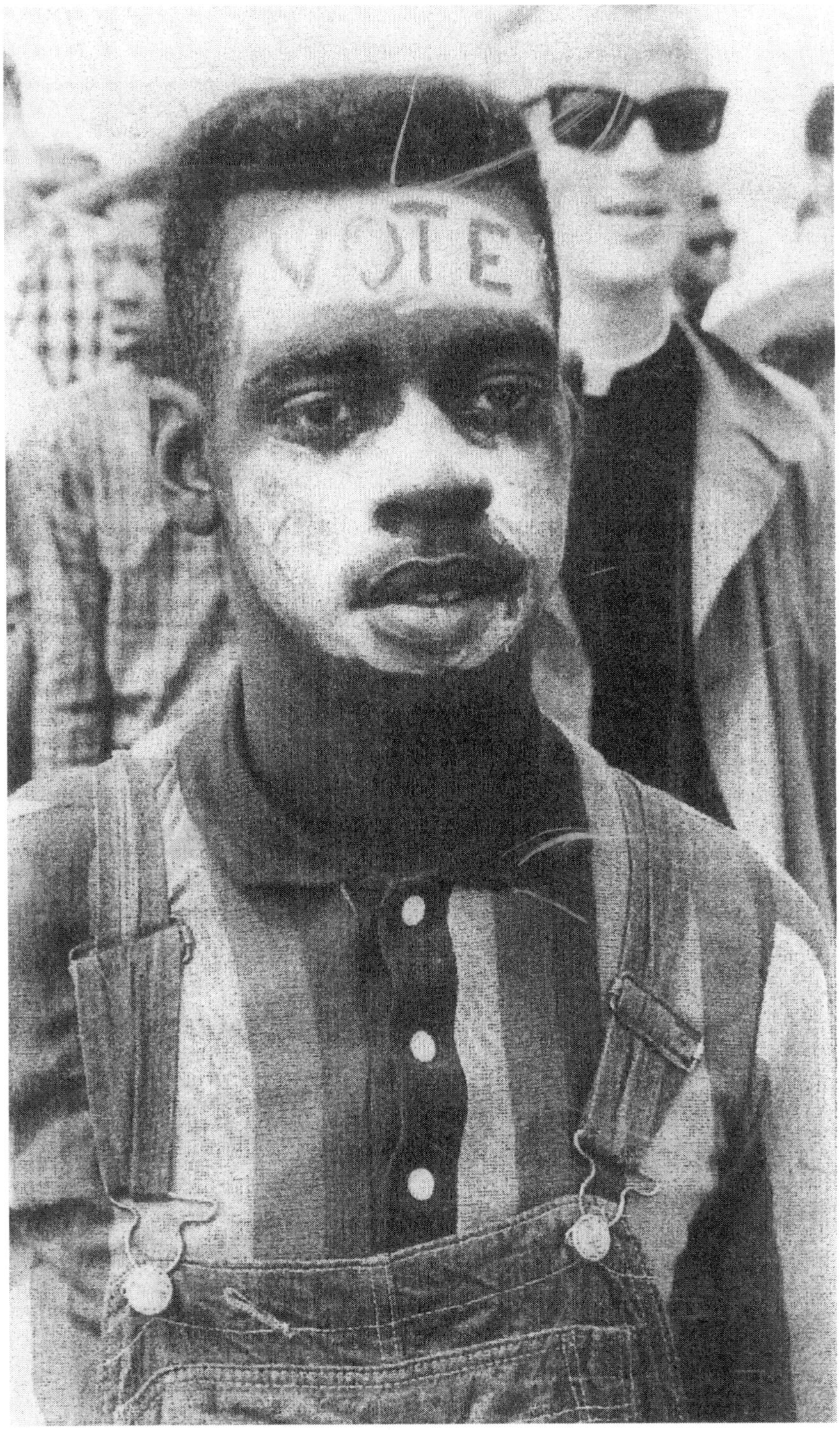
VOTE

Sheriff Jim Clark (R) and Public Safety Director
Wilson Baker Confront Rev. L. L. Anderson (L)

Mary Allen, Carrie Manual,
Johnnie Holloman & Mary Melton

Amelia Boynton, Courageous Eight (Courtesy of the National Voting Rights Museum and Institute)

Marie Foster, Courageous Eight (Courtesy of the National Voting Rights Museum and Institute)

Ernest **Doyle**, Courag
Eight (**Courtesy** of th
National **Voting** Righ
Museum and Institut

The march from Selma to Montgomery, March 1965. Photograph by Peter Pettus,

Selma High School

Carver Apartments Where Henry E. Allen
Fled From Mounted State Troopers

III

On to Tech

I feel like I have been in the midst of a raging storm. My life has not even begun.

Mr. and Mrs. Pepper paid for all my graduation expenses. It is very hard to forget graduation night. None of my family members attended my graduation. I wept tears that ran down my cheeks. For the first time in my life, I felt alone. When I stopped crying, I felt the presence of God. He said, "I will never leave you or forsake you. I will be with you until the end."

I worked all summer and earned sixty-five dollars. I will be buying a one-way bus ticket to Birmingham to attend Wenonah State Technical Institute.

Mr. Pepper wanted me to stay with him so I could help him run the business. Mr. Pepper offered me a paid four-year college education if I went to school in electronics. I said, "No, I need to be my own man." Mr. Pepper said to me, if I ever need any help give him a call. I said to my mother, "I am going off to school." She said to me, "You don't have any money and I don't have any money. Please, please stay at home."

I did not have money for a dormitory. I believed that God would take care of me. The school president gave me a job earning $0.35 an hour. My work schedule was from 4:30 A.M. to 7:00 A.M., operating the school boiler room, using coal with a shovel. I lived in a boarding house. Fifteen of us lived in that house with the owner of the house. We called her "Mommy."

I did janitor work, from cleaning restrooms to mopping the floors upstairs and downstairs.

I also had to wax and buff the floors. I had no income except working for $0.35 per hour. The money that I earned would pay my tuition.

My room and board was $10 per month for an upstairs bunk. I had to buy and cook my own food and wash my own clothes. Every month I would run out of food. My roommates would share food with me. My roommates called me crazy for the $0.35 an hour job. They did not know my financial condition.

I never told anyone about my condition. I just kept my faith in the Lord. I knew he would make a way for me. I was going through some very tough times. Mr. Pepper said to me, if I ever needed anything he would help me. I went through some dark days, but by choice I never called Mr. Pepper.

One afternoon I got so hungry I wanted to cry. I was cleaning the boys' bathroom. The day had passed by and I had no food to eat. I had to tell Jesus that I was hungry, knowing that he already knew. I looked up to heaven and said, "Lord you know that I am hungry. I know that you can give me some food to eat".

I went into the girls' restroom to clean it up. I looked on the wash sink and there lay three quarters. I said, "Thank you, dear Lord." I spoke the word in faith, knowing that you would not stand for your child to go hungry.

I am a living witness that God can make a way out of no way. God will always honor His word. It will not fail and will always come to pass. Trust Him and wait on Him.

I took the three quarters and ran up the hill to the store. I purchased a bag of pot luck cookies. The change I had left over was enough for me to buy a sixteen ounce Topper drink.

When I finished eating, that was the best meal I had ever eaten. Not because of the cookies or drink, I was so happy that the Lord heard my cry and answered my prayers. I will always remember this special meal handed down from heaven. The Lord already knew my need, so he put me in the midst of people that would help meet my need.

Most all my meals were now shared with classmates that live in the boarding house. Mrs. Annie Gooden was a widow and had no children. She was the owner of the house. We all called her Mom. She loved us and we loved her.

On a very cold January evening, an electric heater shorted out in the back bedroom. The house was burning all over before we knew it was on fire. All we could do was run out of the house. When the fire department arrived the house had burned to the ground.

That was a very sad day for all of us that lived in this house. We lost everything we owned. The neighbor gave us a place to sleep. I slept on a concrete floor with no pillow or bedding. The home I lived in, the owner said to me, "I cannot give you any food to eat, but you can claim a spot on the floor." I was very happy to have someplace out of the very cold weather. I slept on the floor for two months.

My floor friend and I decided one Sunday morning to look for the church where all the girls who lived in the dormitory went to church on Sunday. The church was located behind the girls' dorm.

I went and opened the front door to the church and looked in. My eyes made contact with an elderly woman. She said to me, "We are having Youth Sunday, and I would like for you to read a Scripture and pray a prayer."

The lady did not see my floor buddy on the outside of the church. He never looked inside the church. I told my floor buddy, "Let's run." We ran to the top of the hill and stopped. I looked at my friend and said to him, "We must go back to that church."

I was so afraid. My knees were shaking so bad I had to hold them together with my hands. I asked my friend—his name was Tommy—had he ever read a Scripture or prayer in church? He said no. I looked at Tommy and said, "I have never in my life read any Scripture or prayed in church before." Tommy said to me he would read a Scripture if I would pray the prayer. I looked up to heaven and said, "Lord, I don't know, what to say or pray. Please, Lord, help me."

We went back and walked to the church, and the girls' eyes were fixed on Tommy and me. I sat directly in front of the pulpit. I got on my knees and began to pray. The Lord put the words in my mouth to pray. For the very first time in my life, God gave me the will to overcome fear.

From that day on, when I got the call to help with prayer and worship, I could walk in, giving God His glory, and magnify His Holy Name. I knew that the Lord was using me for his purpose only. It had nothing to do with me. God had a plan for my life. He was shaping and molding me for the calling he had on my life.

I would have to face many difficult situations. I was born to be a leader. The Lord had placed a special calling upon me. At Winona State Tech, I was chosen to be president of my class and chairman of the school AAA club.

I started to take notice of myself, and so did my friends. I was checked by some and disliked by others. I had to learn how to accept people even when they did not like me.

I had very little time for pleasure. When I was not working at school, I was earning money ironing clothes at the boarding house for my classmates for $0.25 for shirt or pants.

I made friends with a classmate who lived in Birmingham, Alabama. One Friday night, he invited me to go home with him and meet his family.

He had three sisters and two of them were twins. Anette and Janette. Anette and I became very close friends. Mrs. Michael, their mother, called me Little Henry. Every Friday she would make me cupcakes. The Lord had placed that family in my life to show me love.

My Uncle George, who lived in Bessemer, Alabama, got the news the house where I was living had burned down. My Uncle George asked me, did I want to live with him? I took the offer and moved from Birmingham, Alabama, to Bessemer, Alabama.

I made new friends and joined Mt. Olive Baptist Church. All my new friends attended this church. So I joined the Usher Board and sang in the church choir.

IV

Vietnam Combat

The draft board had given me a two-year deferment to attend Tech for two years. After the graduation, I would be going to the United States Army.

I went and signed up to join the Peace Corps for two years, during the same time the Army had called me. I had to choose between the Peace Corps, which was sending me to the country of India, where I would spend three months at the University of California to learn the Hindu language. It was a great honor to be selected by the United States Government.

The Government of India wrote me a letter explaining the package of benefits the government of India would provide for me—all of my meals and a bicycle, an allowance of five dollars per week, and I could attend the University of India at no cost.

I asked the Peace Corps director, after I completed my two years of duty with the Peace Corps, would I have to go to the Army? He said yes.

I said to the Peace Corps director, "Cancel my tour of duty with the Peace Corps. I am joining the United States Army." The Peace Corps Director said to me, "Send the ticket back to me for your trip to the University of California."

I was inducted into the United States Army from Montgomery, Alabama, on November 29, 1966. I did my basic training at Fort Benning Georgia, located in Columbus, Georgia.

I was assigned to Delta Company, First Training Battalion, located in Sand Hill. I would spend eight weeks there for training. I was told by my commander that I would be in Fort Benning for ten more weeks. The Army wanted me to be a paratrooper. I told my commanding officer that I was drafted by the United States Army; I was not a volunteer.

You have to volunteer to be a paratrooper. Being drafted into the United States Army, you were called a U. S. Soldier. If you volunteered to join the United States Army, you were called an R.A., which means you are Regular Army.

My commander thought that I was a Regular Army soldier. So he volunteered me for eight more weeks of training to become a paratrooper who jumps out of airplanes.

I told my commander, "You cannot volunteer me to be a paratrooper, because I am a draftee not a volunteer."

The commander said to me, "You are correct. I will have your orders changed from Fort Benning Georgia to Fort Polk, Louisiana. Your job will be 11 B-20, an infantry combat soldier." I said, "My God, I do not want to be a fighting soldier." I should have volunteered for the Air Force or Navy for four years.

When I arrived at Fort Polk, Louisiana, there was a big sign posted that read, Tiger Land U.S.A., Little Vietnam. For eight weeks, we went through some of the hardest training your mind and body could endure. We all knew what our next assignment would be—South Vietnam, Jungle warfare.

As a soldier in training, you had to stay focused and maintain a very high level of motivation. The jungle warfare training that we were getting would save your life or your buddy's.

Graduation day finally came. I was given a two-day pass. On April 10, 1967, I boarded a plane at the Montgomery Regional Airport to Fort Dix, New Jersey. On April 10, 1967, I left Fort Dix on a Boeing 707 jet airliner.

My journey would be thirteen thousand miles—over halfway around the world. The plane stopped in Hawaii to refuel. This flight would take 27 hours. The next stop would be the island of Okinawa, Japan. Then to the Republic of South Vietnam.

We landed at the Bien Hoa Air Force Base. The base was located in the city called Long Bien, Vietnam, sixty miles from downtown Saigon. I was now at the Processing Center, where all soldiers leave and return, have to report in or out. The jet airliner brings a load and carries a load back to the U.S.

There were lots of duties at the center. The officer in charge yelled, "I need some volunteer truck drivers." I raised my hand. I was given a wheelbarrow to haul human waste from outdoor toilets. The waste odor made me sick. Human waste is used for rice crops.

I received my orders. I was assigned to the First Infantry Division, called The Big Red One, its nickname. My unit was the First Brigade, First Battalion, Second Infantry, located in Phou Vinh, thirty miles south of Saigon. This battalion was called The Black Scarf Battalion. We wore black scarfs around our necks.

I was assigned to the heavy weapons platoon. My job would be an ammo bearer. I would have to carry 4,000 rounds of ammo for the M-60 machine gun. This big gun needed lots of ammo. This machine gun fires 550 bullets per minute.

I also had to carry my M-16 rifle and all of my equipment. The ammo bearer had the hardest job in the company. No other soldiers wanted to be an ammo bearer. You had to be very physical and tough.

Being a front-line fighting soldier, promotion came very fast. Soldiers were always getting injured or being killed. My first night with the assigned company, we were on night patrol. I was sent out on a listening post to spot the enemy soldier. I saw the enemy soldier and called in and made a report.

We had set up a minefield. The enemy turned the mines around toward us. When my gun crew blew the mines up, one of them got injured. It was the machine gunner who got injured. I was promoted to assistant machine gunner. I no longer carried ammo. I now carried the spare barrel and a .45 caliber pistol.

On another night mission I was at a listening post. We came under attack. The commanding officer called me on the field phone and said, "Hurry back in to my position." The enemy blew up the Claymore mines. My whole gun crew got injured. I did not get injured, thanks to the Lord.

I was now promoted to machine gunner, with a brand-new crew of men. We had to learn to trust each other. It would take some time. I was afraid to trust my assistant gunner. He made my job very hard. I was now sitting here on night watch duty looking for the enemy soldiers.

I was looking back to a few days before when the whole gun crew got injured, and the good Lord had his angels protect me from all harm and danger. The Lord, He is worthy to be praised. He spared my life. I was afraid to allow a soldier to get to be a very close friend. A front-line soldier's life stayed on the line.

I witnessed so many injuries and death. You would talk to a fellow soldier that morning, that evening he would be injured or dead.

I was afraid to get close to anyone. I did not want to face the loss of a dear friend. Two very close friends were playing with each other with their M-16 weapons. One shot the other three times in the chest and killed his best friend. That was a very sad day for all of us. This incident did not happen on the battlefield. It happened back at home base.

We loaded up on helicopters for a search and destroy mission. We unloaded off the helicopters and started walking into a jungle with an open area. One soldier that trained in Fort Polk Jungle Warfare with me stepped on a spring-type mine that blew off one foot. We were in the middle of a minefield.

The first jump in the Vietnam War, and it took place in this minefield. It was done by the 173-Airborne Brigade. They put this minefield in place and did not record the location on the map. Being in the middle of the minefield, not knowing where the hidden mines would be, I looked up to heaven and said, "Lord, please guide us out of this minefield." The Lord heard my prayer. We walked out of the minefield without another soldier being injured. I said, "Thank you, Dear Lord, for your shield of protection. You allow your holy Angels to watch over all of us."

The next day we loaded up on helicopters and went back to home base. Time we arrived back at home base, we came under a rocket attack by the enemy. The tent next to my tent took a direct hit from a rocket.

We all started running for a bunker underground to keep from being injured or killed. It took place late in the evening. It was almost dark. We had problems seeing where we were running to. I could not find an underground bunker to hide in for protection. When I found a bunker, that was all full up with soldiers.

Rockets and mortar rounds fell all around me. There were steel rods in the ground I fell on, some of those rods injuring both of my legs and arms. Three soldiers lost their lives. And many soldiers got injured.

All the other soldiers got their Purple Hearts for battlefield injury. I told my platoon leader I did not want a Purple Heart. My platoon said to me, "You need to take your Purple Heart." I told my platoon leader the answer was still no.

We had orders to go and clear the main highway to Saigon. When the road was clear of road bombs, the truck convoys could move out supplies. We used a mine sweeper to find hidden bombs and landmines in the roadway.

We had finished clearing the road and were waiting for the helicopter to pick us up. I stopped and chatted with a fellow soldier. We talked for about ten minutes, and I walked to the landing area. I heard a loud explosion, flesh and blood flew in my direction. I heard screaming and crying. I did not want to look back behind me, because I knew something real bad had taken place.

The soldier that I had just finished talking to had a hand grenade pin worked loose, and he did not know it. The M-25 frag grenade had a nine-second fuse on it. The explosion killed him and two soldiers that were standing beside him, and injured several other soldiers. After that bad incident I looked in my hand grenade pouch to check my three M-25 hand grenades. One of my pins had worked loose. I carefully put the pin back in place and said, "Lord, I thank you so much. Time after time, you have spared my life."

We had been in the jungle for over three months, looking for the enemy soldiers. The name of our operation was Billinsley Search and Destroy. My body was covered with bloodsucking leeches. I picked them up when I crossed the muddy rivers and streams.

My cloth jungle fatigues had rotted on my body. This was during the rainy season, called the monsoon season. It would rain every day. My company finally stopped, so we could get the leeches off each other.

The bloodsucking leeches would bury their head into your flesh. If you pull the leaches out of your flesh, you would leave the head still buried in your flesh. That would cause a very bad infection to your flesh. I carried four pounds of explosive called composition C-4. This explosive would burn the leeches, and they would back out of your flesh.

The only time we took a bath was with rainwater. I would stand in the rain with a bar of soap. I would wash my jungle fatigues that I was wearing and my body at the same time.

We never had much water to drink. We were walking through the jungle and spotted a coconut tree. We were told that green coconuts had water inside of them. One of the soldiers climbed a coconut tree and threw down all the green coconuts. We found one drop of water in each coconut.

Drinking water was very limited. Most of us did not have any water to drink. We slept in mud like water buffalo. We wore our uniforms until they rotted on our bodies.

I kept a towel to cover up my M-60 machine gun during the rainy season to keep it dry, because when I needed it to fire, I wanted the M-60 machine gun to be ready. The M-60 machine gun was my wife and I was the husband. We were married to each other through the good and bad times, we had to stick together. Only God, my Father in Heaven, could see me through these dark days.

It was almost night and time for me to clean my M-60 machine gun. I was very tired from carrying that twenty-four pound gun, crawling through the tough and dense jungle all day, searching for the enemies. The machine gun has a spring, located in part of the operating rod handle. This spring, when the machine was in the firing position, carried three hundred pounds of pressure loaded.

I made a very bad and costly mistake of not placing the operating rod handle bolt in the forward position that would remove the pressure of the spring guide. When I took the yoke off that holds the spring in place, the spring popped out, hitting me in the center of my chest cavity. It almost knocked me to the ground.

My chest was hurting me real bad. I was afraid that my heart was injured. I was sent out of the jungle by helicopter back to base camp, so that I could get a flight by airplane to an Army field hospital for a chest x-ray.

The field hospital was located at a location sixty miles from the area I just left, the Army field hospital located in the town of Lai Khe. This field hospital was the central location where all wounded soldiers would go.

I boarded an old World War II twin-engine airplane. When the plane left the runway from Division Headquarters located in the town of Dien, the plane began to climb. When the pilot arrived at the level the plane would travel, the right engine went dead.

The airplane pilot said to me, "This plane cannot stay at this height." Only the pilot and I were on that plane. The pilot said to me, "I can fly this plane with one engine, but we will be flying treetops, very low and the plane will be flying sideways."

We were flying over enemy territory. We did not have the helicopter gunship escort. I began to pray, asking the Lord for his protection to guide this plane to a safe landing. The Lord heard my prayer, the plane landed safely on the Lai Khe airstrip.

I went to the hospital and had my chest x-ray. I received good news from the doctor. My heart was not damaged. I did receive some torn cartilage in my chest cavity.

I got a double blessing from the Lord. He allowed the plane to land safely and my heart was all right. Thank you, dear Lord, for your round-the-clock protection. My assigned Guardian Angel was always keeping watch over me. Time after time, the Lord has made a way out of no way for me.

As a fighting man, we had problems seeing in the dense jungles in the daylight hours. We were going out on our first night operation. This was a very dangerous assignment. We could very easily shoot each other. I took my position in the midst of bamboo. I got tired of standing and kneeling and decided to sit down, not knowing where I was sitting.

I sat down on a poisonous scorpion. I got stung in my rear end. My whole backside was in pain. I cried out for the medic to help me. I was so afraid that I would die. I looked up to heaven and said, "Lord, please don't let me die." The Lord heard my cry and did not allow the scorpion sting to kill me. Thank you, dear Lord. That was a night I will never forget.

The First Brigade of the First Infantry Division had received orders for the largest search and destroy mission ever conducted. The operation was called operation Billinsley. This operation would last for 120 days. This is how long we would stay in the jungle.

I was now loading on the helicopter with my M-60 machine gun: one hundred rounds of ammo in my gun, one hundred packed on my back. My weight was so heavy, I needed help loading onto the helicopter. The helicopter took us to an unknown location and dropped us off.

We walked for several miles to get to our campsite. We finally arrived at the site. I needed some camouflage to hide my M-60 machine gun position from the enemy. I went to find bamboo. When I arrived at the location, another soldier was there gathering some bamboo for camouflage. We began to talk while we cut bamboo.

All of a sudden a bamboo viper snake crawled out on a piece of bamboo and bit the soldier on the hand. Standing next to me, he cried out. I called for the medic. It was very hot and humid that day. In a matter of minutes he was dead. I did not know what to say or do. The bamboo viper is one of the world's worst poisonous snakes. I could have been bitten very easily. We were both standing side-by-side, talking and cutting stalks of bamboo. The viper could have very easily bitten me instead of him.

It took me quite a while to get over this event. I was seeking the correct answer. No man could answer that question for me, only the Father in Heaven could reveal the right answer to me. The Lord's guardian angel stood between me and death. God has all power, even if the viper had bitten me. If it was God's will for me to live, the viper bite would not have been death.

Later in the day, the company went out on patrol, looking for the enemy. I was very hot and thirsty, needing some water very badly. We crossed the river by holding onto a rope. When we crossed over to the other side, we came to a rice paddy where the rice was grown. The Vietnamese people used human waste or fertilize their crops.

I saw a clean stream of water in the rice paddy. We all carry some water purification tablets in our canteen pouch. Anyone who would drink any of this contaminated water did not expect to live. You would contract the liver disease called hepatitis and die. I looked up to heaven and said, "Lord, you know that I need some water to drink. I am going to drink this water in your name." The Word of God said, if you have a mustard seed of faith you can tell a mountain, be thou removed. I stepped out in faith, believing that God was going to bless that water, and he did.

After filling my stomach with water, I said, "Thank you, dear Lord, I am depending on you." The Lord is my light and salvation. Whom shall I fear? The Lord is the strength of my life. Who shall be afraid? Many of my fellow soldiers drank some bad water and contracted hepatitis and died.

We had now been in the jungle for 60 days. We were in the midst of the rainy season called the monsoon. It would rain every day. We wore jungle boots without socks. We stayed on the move, looking for the enemy. The name of the operation is Search and Destroy. Our feet stayed wet for long periods of time.

There is a disease in this part of the world is called jungle rot. Your foot would crack open and turn real dark. Many soldiers got this disease because they didn't pull their jungle boots off when we made a rest stop. Every time the company made a rest stop, I would take off my boots and dry my feet with my hands. By doing this, it stopped my feet from getting jungle rot. However I did get an infection from bloodsucking leech bites.

It was now time to move to another area. We stayed on the go. We moved by helicopter. The jungle was so dense and thick it was very hard to move. I spent my days having to crawl on my knees with my M-60 machine gun, which weighed 24 pounds dry and more when I got wet.

The helicopter finally arrived and took us to another area where the enemy was hiding, and dropped us off in an enemy base camp unknowingly. The helicopter came under heavy weapons fire.

One helicopter was shot down by enemy fire. The helicopter that I was riding on also came under fire. The pilots refused to set the chopper down. I was 20 feet in the air. The door gunner pushed me out of the helicopter 20 feet in the air. I landed in the middle of a rice paddy and sunk waist deep in mud. I said, "Lord, I cannot go any further."

My assistant gunner, who was to my right side, got shot in the upper shoulder. My ammo bearer to my left side got shot in the chest area. I was to carry the whole load. I just lost my assistant gunner and one ammo bearer. What am I going to do?

We were in a firefight in the enemy house. Bullets were flying all over the area. We had to call in for air support.

We fought the enemy for hours. Several of our soldiers lost their lives in this battle. I never knew whether my two crew members lived or died. We didn't get this kind of information.

We defeated the enemy. It was time to move again. We were waiting on the helicopter to arrive. We loaded up on a helicopter headed for base camp.

That helicopter had a load master called a door gunner. His weapon was an M-60 machine gun. His job was to make sure that the helicopter was not overloaded. We all boarded the helicopter. The helicopter made a takeoff. It went straight up into the air, and came down to the ground and crashed.

Several soldiers got injured in the crash of the helicopter. I carried more weight than any other soldier on board. I carried my M-60 machine gun, four thousand rounds of ammo and the spare barrel to the machine gun. I had to carry all this equipment, because I had lost my whole crew. They had earlier been shot by enemy soldiers.

In the midst of this helicopter crash, I did not receive a scratch. I said, "Thank you, dear Lord, for allowing your Guardian Angels to place a protective shield all around me. Thank you, Father in Heaven, for all the things you continue to do for me," You can search the whole world over, and you will find nobody like Him. He is God all by himself. Glory to His holy name.

I always kept a small Bible in my left front pocket, wrapped in plastic, so I could keep it dry from monsoon rain. My favorite passage was Psalm 27; this passage gave me my daily spiritual food and medicine to my soul.

I had a new machine gun crew. We are having a time getting to trust each other. My unit is on the move again, looking for the enemy.

In a secret command meeting, I was chosen to be part of a ten-man team. We would be taken by helicopter to an unknown location. The unit commander did not tell us that we would be bait for the enemy. The commander expected all ten of us to be killed by the enemy.

Late that afternoon, the helicopter came and picked us up, and dropped us off in the jungle. I said to all the soldiers, "We are going to set up a night perimeter." I had forty thousand rounds of ammo. I was going to set up my M-60 machine gun to cover the right and left flanks, and all nine M-16 rifles would be in position. After that, we set up our Claymore mines. We put trip flares in place for early warning devices to detect the enemy.

I said to the other soldiers, "I am not planning on being killed." If only one man makes it out alive, it will be me. I stayed awake all night, talking to the Lord and watching for the enemy. God blessed us and kept us safe throughout the night. We have a God that is real.

The next morning it was very early and the day had just begun. The First Battalion 2nd Infantry arrived. There were Headquarters Company, Alpha, Bravo, Charlie and Delta Company. To their surprise, we were still alive and well. The enemy knew that we were bait and chose not to attack a small band of soldiers.

Not knowing all the facts, we were set up less than a quarter-mile from the enemy base camp of Vietnamese regular soldiers from North Vietnam, who had made their way down south.

Two companies of U.S. soldiers lined up in two files to move out. Find and destroy the enemy. The First Battalion 2nd Infantry sent our recon platoon ahead of the two other companies. The enemy was very smart. They let the recon platoon pass through. Bravo Company was the lead company. I was in the second company—Charlie Company. The enemy had set up a horseshoe ambush for Bravo Company.

Bravo Company walked into this horseshoe ambush. The enemy opened fire on Bravo Company. They had no way to go or hide. Bravo Company lost 175 men in this battle.

Charlie Company, my company, moved into battle with the North Vietnamese regulars. Men were dying and getting injured all around me. I moved my M-60 machine gun online. I fired over thirty thousand rounds of ammo in this major battle. I burned up three M-60 machine guns. I fired until the barrels got so hot they would melt.

This battle went on for several hours. The United States had an aircraft carrier stationed in the South China Sea. F-105 jet planes were stationed on this carrier. These jets were used to give us air support on bombing missions.

We were pinned down by the enemy. We could not move. The enemy could not move. We were almost on top of each other, almost hand-to-hand combat. The artillery F.0. Officer called for air support. The F-105 jets were carrying bombs under each wing.

I was looking when the jet pilot released a 150-pound bomb. The bomb was headed right on top of me and my crew. The bomb hit a tree and exploded and sent hot metal in all directions. Some hot metal went down in my pants and stopped on my bottom. I said to my assistant gunner, "Please look and see whether or not I have a behind. My whole back went numb. My assistant gunner looked at me and laughed and said to me, "Your ass is still there."

We had soldiers being killed by the enemy and air support. We were so close to each other. The company medic was behind me. A fellow soldier got shot. The medic left me to help a wounded soldier. He was killed.

My platoon leader said to me that I needed to move my M-60 machine gun to cover the right flank. I would be moving into an area where there was no protection from the enemy.

I knelt down on my knees and asked the Lord to protect me when I moved. I moved in a very low crouch position. I placed my M-60 machine gun underneath my arm and moved as fast as I could.

The enemy had located my machine gun position. Their plan was to take me out. The reason why they wanted to take me out was because my M-60 machine gun would fire 550 bullets per minute. When I moved into the open area, so many enemy soldiers shot at me so many times.

When I hit the ground, I started feeling my body, looking for bullet holes in my body. I found no bullet holes in my body. All I wanted to say was, "Thank you, dear Lord, were saving my life." My Guardian Angel got between me and those enemy bullets and spared my life.

We lost so many soldiers from death and injuries, I became very angry and bitter. All I wanted to do was look for the enemy. Find them and kill them with my M-60 machine gun. The injuries and deaths to my fellow soldiers had turned to me into a madman.

All I wanted to do was count the enemy's dead bodies. I was playing the role of a bounty hunter, taking no live prisoners. Thank God for Jesus, who picked me up and turned me around when I needed him most. I had lost all my feeling to love and care. Our air support had dropped many bombs on the enemy soldiers. Over 500 bodies were counted. They were left for three days.

My fellow soldiers searched the dead enemy soldier bodies. They found photos of wives and children and other family members. God gave me a chance to see what had happened to me. This M-60 machine gun and the war had taken a toll on me. I needed help, and only God could restore all that I had lost. We were fighting on different sides, but we were still brothers in the sight of God.

They picked us up and we moved to another enemy location. We were in and out of battles with enemy soldiers when the brigade went out on a major search and destroy mission. We were very strong because we consisted of three battalions of infantry soldiers. You are looking at over 1,000 soldiers.

We were now waiting for helicopters to arrive and carry us to another enemy location. The helicopter dropped us off in the midst of the enemy camp. We were fighting so close to the enemy. It was like hand-to-hand combat.

My gun crew drew heavy fire from the enemy. Three of our soldiers lost their lives. My platoon leader called for air support from our helicopter gunships. They fired grenade rockets and 20-millimeter guns.

I was in charge of the radio that was called a prick-25 radio. The helicopter pilot called me on the radio and said, "Throw a smoke grenade to mark your location." I had three smoke grenades. I threw a yellow smoke grenade. The wind was so high and clouds were so low, you could touch the clouds with your hands. The helicopter pilot called me and said, "I do not see your yellow smoke to mark your location." The pilot said to me, "Throw another yellow smoke grenade." I said to the pilot, "I don't have another smoke grenade to throw." The helicopter pilot said to me, "I am coming in firing."

Rockets and bullets fell all around me. I got on my knees and put my head to the ground and committed my soul to the Lord. I held my own funeral. I knew that my life had come to the end. The Lord placed his holy Angels in the midst of those rockets and bullets. I looked up to heaven and said, "Lord, I thank you for saving my life. Time after time you have made death behave."

I have finally made my one year and am ready to go back to base camp and start processing out of the Republic of South Vietnam. My first night at base camp, this camp came under heavy rocket and mortar attacks. I was supposed to run into the bunker next to mine, but in front, but I ran out back and fell headfirst into the bunker.

Six soldiers were standing on my back. I could not say a word. My lower back was injured. The doctor told me that he would have to extend my tour of duty in Vietnam. I said to the doctor, "Please don't extend my tour of duty. I will get my back x-rayed in the United States." I did not want to spend another night in this place. The doctor cleared me to come home.

Several soldiers, including me, were loaded up on a two-and-a-half-ton truck and taken to Bien Hoa Air Force Base to depart to Travis Air Force Base located in Oakland, California. We loaded on a big commercial Boeing 707 airplane. As the plane began to taxi along the runway, the enemy fired rockets and mortar rounds on the runway, trying to hit the airplane.

I looked out the airplane window and could see rockets and mortar rounds as they hit the runway. I began praying to the Lord, "Please don't let this plane get shot down by those rockets and mortar rounds." When the big plane left the runway and started climbing into the air, I said, "Lord, thank you so much for hearing my prayers."

After twenty-seven hours of airtime, we landed at Travis Air Force Base. I got off the plane and kissed the runway and promised the Good Lord that I would serve Him for the rest of my life. I am committed to what I promised God, even though from time to time I have strayed from the path. My life has nothing to do with me. It is all about my Lord and Savior Jesus Christ. All the glory and honor belong to Him.

I returned home to historic Selma, Alabama, on November 29, 1968. I was discharged from the United States Army. My last duty station was Fort Hood, Texas. Because of the Vietnam War, I chose not to remain in the United States Army.

Fort Hood left me with very bad memories. There was so much racism going on at the time in the U. S. Military just back from the war. I did not expect to come back home and face what was left behind me. Black soldiers wearing black arm bands on their wrists. And refusing to go to Chicago Civil Duty Patrol.

This took place at the Democratic Convention in 1968, Chicago. The Black soldiers that refused the order to go were placed in the stockade. All those soldiers were just back from Vietnam.

I did not support the black soldiers' efforts, because they went about things the wrong way. I was trying very hard to adjust back to normal life. I struggled very hard within myself. I had lost all of my human touch and feeling. I felt so lost and out of touch with life. I asked the Lord, "Where do I go from here?"

The Lord had already delivered me from the snares of the war. Why was I so afraid? I chose to go my own way, leaving the Lord out of my life. God allowed me to go through many struggles because of my hard heart.

I was on my own mission and getting nothing done. I became angry and told God two things I was not going to be. I was not going to Preach and Teach. God continued to let me wander in the desert, I went from job to job and happy at nothing that I was doing. I finally came to myself and asked God what is it that He wanted me to do. I did not get a quick answer from God. He made me wait on him.

V

First Black in Selma Fire Department

The city of Selma is known for its history. 1865, the Battle of Selma between the North and the South. One hundred years later, the 1965 march across the world famous Edmund Pettus Bridge was known as Bloody Sunday. In August 1965, the Voters Rights Act was passed, giving all Americans the Right To Vote.

In 1972, I, Henry E. Allen, became the first black to be hired as a firefighter in the city of Selma. Growing up in a segregated society, there was no way possible to dream of being a firefighter. Thank you, Dear Lord, for choosing me.

This the second time that the Lord has given me a call. Less than a year earlier, the Lord had called me to integrate the Alabama National Guard. Now I am being used by the Lord to tear down racial barriers in the Selma Fire Department.

Lord, I thank You for giving me the assignment. You could have chosen someone else to carry out Your mission. The city of Selma Fire Chief L. B. Jones came to my house and told me to follow him to his office, located at 1500 Broad Street, Number Three Fire Station.

Chief Jones left me at the fire house without telling me that I had been hired to be a firefighter.

The Station Captain's name was Whitaker, and the driver's name was Smith. He drove the fire engine. Captain Whitaker asked me, when did I plan to eat? I said to Captain Whitaker, "I will eat when I get home." He said to me, "You won't get off until 7:00 A.M. in the morning."

Captain Whitaker allowed me to drive home for food and clothes. When I returned back to the fire house, the fire alarm went off. Sims Lumber Company had a large building on fire. When we arrived on the fire scene, the old building was falling to the ground. Assistant Chief Dreamus told me to get on top of that burning building. I told him that the roof was falling in, and I was not going on top of that old building. Captain Whitaker said to me, "You made the right decision."

I was assigned to Number One Fire Station on C Shift. This shift was called the click shift, because the assistant chief and the station captain were the city of Selma mayor's war buddies. The mayor's office was located in the same building that housed Number One Fire Station, where I was assigned.

The firefighters at this location had their way. They were able to get away with rule violations that other stations could not get away with. The mayor protected them, they answered only to the mayor.

I spent most of my time studying my Bible and reading firefighter manuals.

These special men were allowed to get drunk on duty and earn extra money while on fire department payroll.

The Lord had placed me in the fire department for his purpose, not my own. At that time I did not know what all the Lord had in store for me to do. I continued to obey the Lord and did my very best on the job.

My work schedule was 24 hours on duty and 24 hours off duty, time 1:00 A.M. to 7:00 A.M. I was on probation for one year. I had to work with every fire house in the department, because I was the swing man.

Every fire house I went to, they would have extra work for me to do, or special details waiting for me. My white brothers handled me very carefully and with a lot of respect.

One station captain refused to speak to me for three months. I found out what his problem was. It had nothing to do with me. He was afraid to let me know that he could not read and write very well. His learning skills were very poor.

My starting salary was $390.00 per month. This was a very low salary for me. I had worked for United Parcel Service and CXS Rail Road. I continued to trust in the Lord, knowing that he would supply all of my needs.

I went and purchased a Reference Bible that would help me get a better understanding of God's Word. This Bible was bought in 1972. I still have this Bible.

All firefighters had to pull phone watch, answering emergency fire calls. When I pulled the last half of phone watch all the firefighters were asleep. I would take this quiet time learning how to operate the fire engine and fire pump, simulating how to operate the fire apparatus.

At that time what little knowledge firefighters had they would not share. Most of the firefighters had very little education or none at all.

We received a fire call in our district: a car was on fire. For some strange reason the driver of the fire engine asked me, did I want to drive the fire engine back to the fire house. Knowing that I had received no training on operating this piece of equipment, the driver had no idea that I had been training myself. The driver was trying to make me look bad.

I moved over into the driver's seat and took off driving the fire engine. The driver looked at me and said, "I know that no one has taught you to drive this truck. I am going to teach you everything I know about this fire engine."

On December 17, 1973, I got promoted to firefighter driver, assigned to Number Four Station, located at 800 Cahaba Road. I worked at this station for seven years.

This station was called the slow station, because it did not make many fire calls. For that reason, I wanted to be moved to another fire house. In the year of 1977, I was promoted to fire lieutenant and was still at the same fire house. The fire lieutenant from Number Two Fire House wanted to be moved. The two of us were allowed to swap with each other.

My move took place in the midst of an ongoing investigation in the Selma Fire Department that involved the fire chief and the assistant chief. The assistant chief pleaded guilty to wrongdoing. The chief said that he knew nothing about the wrongdoing.

The investigation centered around the mayor. Because the fire chief refused to plead guilty, he was demoted from fire chief to fire inspector. This move left the fire chief job open. The mayor was a dictator, and all the Fire Department senior officers were afraid to apply for the chief job.

VI

Advancement to Fire Chief

I, Henry E. Allen, a young junior officer, applied for the chief job. The mayor said that I was too young to handle the fire chief's job and brought in a detective from the Police Department and tried to appoint him chief. I told the Public Safety Committee he could not be called fire chief. So they called him fire administrator.

After the former police detective had become fire administrator, the mayor named his son Head of the Detective Division. For the first time in the history of the Selma Fire Department, we didn't have a fire chief.

This decision, made by the mayor, made senior fire officers in the Fire Department look very stupid with no leadership ability. Blacks and whites who were not a part of his system faced tough times under the mayor's leadership. The fire administrator followed a similar pattern, except he discriminated against all the black firefighters. Several years had gone by; he showed no changes in racism.

The Spirit of the Lord guided me to pay him a visit. I went into his office and greeted him. I told him that he was being very unfair to all the blacks that worked in the Selma Fire Department. "And I demand that you stop discriminating against blacks."

I told him that he had segregated the department. He had placed all the blacks on one shift and set aside certain pieces of equipment only whites could operate. When I had finished speaking, he looked at me very strangely and said to me, "I am sorry. I will make the changes you ask me to make." It was not me speaking, it was God speaking through me. I give God the glory.

The city council had passed a resolution for a state retirement plan. Four fire captains retired in thirty days, leaving four captain slots open. Five captains will be competing for the four positions. Four whites and one black captain.

The four white captains were given a copy of the captain exam by the personnel director. A white brother informed me of what had taken place. I went home and prayed to the Lord, asking him to guide me in what I needed to do.

I wrote a letter to the city council president and listed all the violations that had taken place involving the captain exam. I wanted to meet with the mayor and the city council. The president refused to grant me a meeting with the council on these issues.

I told the council president that I was going to file a race discrimination charge against the City of Selma mayor, personnel director and the fire administrator. These charges were filed with the Equal Employment Opportunity Commission (EEOC) in Birmingham, Alabama.

After the ongoing investigation was completed by the EEOC, the City of Selma was found guilty of the charges. The City of Selma admitted to the wrongdoing charges and asked for an agreement to correct the problems.

Part of the agreement by the EEOC and the city of Selma was to pay Auburn University three hundred and fifty thousand dollars to set up a test program for all public safety employees. The Lord heard and answered my prayer. Thank you, dear Lord.

This was a landmark decision for all city employees, giving everyone a fair and equal chance to compete for jobs working for the City of Selma.

When Auburn University administered the first captain test, I passed and was promoted to captain. Through all the danger that was around me, God said, No Weapons That Are Formed Against Me Shall Prosper. Those Holy Angels Kept Watch Over Me, keeping me free of harm and danger. I was not afraid to take a bold stand for the things that were right.

At that time I was still in the Alabama National Guard. In May of 1991, I was attending annual training at Camp Shelby, Mississippi, training for the Persian Gulf War. I was running and fell into a hole. I injured my arms and bruised my left rib cage and my left ankle.

It took fifteen months for me to heal. In the meantime, the personnel director would call the National Guard, trying to find a way to hurt me because of the charges I filed against the City of Selma. I had a broken ankle and torn ligament in my left ankle. I asked the military doctors to give me a medical release, so that I could return back to work. The doctors gave me the medical release.

The City of Selma would not allow me to return back to work unless I had a heart stress test. When I was off work for an ankle injury, I had to go to Birmingham, Alabama, to the Heart Clinic. The only reason you would go to this clinic was for a heart attack or heart bypass surgery, and I had neither one.

I prayed to the Lord all the way to Birmingham. I passed the heart stress test. The Kirkland Clinic doctors said to me, "We tried to give you a heart attack, your heart is in good condition." I said to the doctors, "Fax my medical report back to Family Medical in Selma, Alabama, so I can return back to work."

I knew what was in store for me at my job. I would continue to do my job to the best of my ability and ask the Lord to keep me covered from my enemies, who were trying to take me out.

A position for battalion chief had come open because of retirement. I was the senior captain and the most qualified firefighter. It came as no surprise to me, the hatred the Mayor had toward me. Everyone knew it. He gave the job to one of his cronies over me. I did not say a word to anyone. I just kept my faith in the Lord and quoted a passage of Scripture which said, If God Be For Me Who Can Be Against Me And Prevail.

The next year the Lord appointed me to be the assistant chief. The fire administrator was relieved of his duties. I was given the authority over all the Fire Department personnel matters. God said, The Steps Of A Good Man Are Ordered By The Lord.

The fire administrator already disliked me, and now that I was in charge of all Fire Department personnel, he really showed himself. I made my office in a room in the firefighters' dormitory. The whole department was very excited about me over personnel. The administrator shared one thing with me, "Don't turn your back on anyone, I had to learn the hard way. And good luck to you."

The Selma Fire Department had to be built from ground zero. The Lord sent me all the help that I needed from Birmingham Fire Chief Oscar Brennan. Chief Brennan gave me all the information that I needed to start rebuilding the Selma Fire Department.

It was going to take some long hours to get this job done. The building process had just begun. The mayor did not know that the good Lord had ordained me for this job. The mayor tried everything in his power to make me humble myself to him. All other department heads were afraid of the mayor accept me.

In the meantime, there was an investigation going on in the city of Selma by the state and federal government. The police chief and the city clerk had stolen over $1 million from the general fund budget. I turned some documents over to the FBI.

I asked a council member not to tell anyone about the information that I had shared with him because my life could be in danger. That councilman betrayed me in a public meeting by telling the audience that the information I had given him broke the case wide open.

Someone from that meeting went and told the mayor that I was a key player in the investigation. I had turned in very important information to the FBI. The mayor went after me, trying to discredit me, accusing me of wrongdoing.

I had gotten permission from the city clerk to purchase several pieces of home entertainment units, five for the firehouse and two for me. The city clerk had said to me, "It will be all right for you to make the purchase." I said to her, "I am buying a money order to cover my order."

When the mayor called the clerk into his office and asked, did she tell me that it was all right to make the purchase, she told the mayor that she knew nothing about the purchase. She lied in my face. That was the worst I had ever faced. For her lie, I got suspended for two weeks without pay.

I stayed home fasting and praying. I had been lied on. I was very hurt. I received a call from one of my prayer partners, who said to me "I know that it is hard for you to believe what I am about to say. I am your friend."

Being a white brother and telling a black brother that you are his friend can be hard to believe, coming from a white male. My brother said to me, "What can I do to help you?"

He told me that God had given him a message to share with me, and he tried not to carry it out. The Lord gave him no peace until he called me.

The message was taken from Isaiah 43:2, When Thou Passest Through The Waters, I Will Be With Thee; And Through The Rivers, They Shall Not Overflow Thee: When Thou Walkest Through The Fire, Thou Shalt Not Be Burned; Neither Shall The Flame Kindle Upon Thee.

When I received that message, it gave me all the hope and courage that I needed.

The Lord Promised Never To Leave Me Nor Forsake Me. The Lord Said They That Wait Upon The Lord Shall Renew Their Strength. They Shall Mount Up With Wings As An Eagle. They Shall Run And Not Get Weary, They Shall Walk And Not Faint. All The Glory And Honor Belong To The Lord.

Returning back to work with a clean heart and a new spirit, in spite of all that had happened, it was for my good. I had so much to thank the Lord for. He had chosen me to be the First Black Fire Chief of The Selma Fire Department. He could have chosen someone else to carry out His mission. But he used me. Lord, I Thank You For Allowing Me To Serve.

Serving for twenty-seven years under the leadership of Mayor Joseph T. Smitherman was a very tough job. Every move that was made was based on your relationship with him. I kept my trust in the Lord. Mayor Joe T. Smitherman sent me a message by two council members. The message that the mayor sent was, "When are you going to join my team? I want you to stop trying to be a man and be a boy."

I looked at both of the black councilmen and asked them the question, "What do you want me to do?" They would not answer my question. I said to the both of them, "Go back and tell Mayor Smitherman I am trying too hard to be a man. I don't know how to be a boy."

The councilmen became very angry with me. I knew that the message I gave the two councilmen would bring real hardship upon me. I was not afraid of what would happen, because God was on my side.

One Councilman brought me the message from the mayor, saying that the mayor was giving all department heads a seven percent raise. I will not be getting one. Mayor Smitherman also said as long as he is mayor, I would never get a pay increase.

That was fine with me. Working for the city of Selma and being an outsider, not an insider, was a hard job. Other department heads were afraid to talk with me in the presence of the mayor. The mayor finally called me to his office.

The mayor knew that I did not fear him at all. He had two black department heads in his office. They listened while the mayor talked to me. I was a thorn in his side. Every department head in the city of Selma, he had them under his wing.

The mayor said to me, "You think that I am a real redneck? I did not respond to his question. He said to me again, "You think that I am a real redneck? He said to me, "Ask the department heads, they will tell you that I am not a redneck."

I already knew that the mayor was not redneck, he was a dictator, who wanted to rule and control everybody. He was very much in control. He controlled the city with an iron hand. He was feared by both blacks and whites.

The mayor did not like me, but he gave me the highest respect. He knew that I was a very good and strong leader. That was all that I wanted from him. What God put in place, man cannot move. My only hope was to stay prayerful.

The Selma Fire and Rescue Department still continued to grow in spite of all the things that we were facing: taking money out of my budget and giving it to the Police Department. The Selma Fire Department never had enough funds to operate with. Through it all every year, the Lord always brought us through.

In the summer of the year of 2000, the city of Selma purchased its first area platform ladder truck since the year of 1967. This piece of equipment was a real classic. It took a long time to get the mayor and city council to purchase this piece of equipment. The city passed a bond, and paid $555,000 to pay for this piece of equipment. I went to a week-long grant writing school in Montgomery, Alabama, to learn how to write proposals and grants.

Two railroads had tracks that ran through the heart of Selma. We have Norfolk Southern and the Meridian Railroad. I sent a proposal to Norfolk Southern's home office in Norfolk Virginia, and asked for funds to put together a HazMat team in Selma, Alabama. Norfolk's home office said to me, "We can only give you some hazmat software. Your town is too small to give you grant money." The other railroad refused to answer my request.

The city of Selma is a small community. Both railroads route all of the worst chemicals through this city day and night. Being the fire chief and knowing that all these dangerous chemicals were passing through twenty-four hours per day, it troubled me greatly. The fire chief was responsible to the people for their safety.

Having the knowledge that any one of these tank cars that transport these hazardous chemicals could derail in the city, causing the loss of many lives, I went back to the mayor and city council, and gave them the figures of what it would cost to put a hazmat unit in place. The mayor and council applauded me for my efforts to get a HazMat unit. I was told in a sad voice, "We know the needs. We do not have the money." I said quietly, "I am not going to give up."

I went to the emergency Management director and asked the homeland security director, "What could we do, not as the city of Selma but as Dallas County?" The emergency management director gave me some good news. Homeland Security would give us a thirty-five–foot HazMat trailer. We would have to buy a truck to pull it. My crying out, the Lord heard my cry.

One more hill to climb, getting the city and county to agree on this HazMat trailer. The city and county had problems working together. I met with the mayor of Selma and got permission to meet with the Dallas County probate judge. Both governments must agree to pay fifty/fifty. They did agree.

The city of Selma and Dallas County had its first ever HazMat unit: a thirty-five–foot trailer, fully equipped. We did not have a truck at that time to pull the thirty-five–foot trailer. We had to use our battalion chief wagon to pull the trailer. At a later date, the emergency management director received a grant from Homeland Security, and purchased a truck.

In order to have a HazMat team, you must have a HazMat tech. I sent my company officer to Alabama State Fire College for training. The HazMat had to pass the state certified exam. The goal was to have a twelve-man team. The HazMat could face very dangerous situations from time to time. I had to ask for volunteers who wanted to serve as a HazMat techs.

The HazMat techs' job was to go into the hot area of a chemical spill with their Level #4 chemical suit on and with a chemical detector monitor, find out what type of chemical had spilled. It was a hard task to keep volunteers on the team.

During the same time, I was a student in the National Fire Academy, located in Emmitsburg, Maryland, in Public Safety for Firefighters. The Fire Academy was as high as you could go. This Academy was a part of Howard University. This was very tough, but I made it through.

Most cities large or small had a fire marshal in their department, except the city of Selma. One of my main goals was to get the city of Selma to make funds available in my budget to bring aboard a fire marshal. It failed. My next move was to send all my company fire officers to the Alabama State Fire College to become fire investigators. It worked out very well. All my company officers were fire investigators.

I wrote my very first grant, called the Fire Grant. We received a total of $269,000. Much needed equipment was purchased: fire fighting equipment, self-contained breathing apparatuses—used to enter buildings filled with smoke—and an air machine used to fill air bottles.

We also obtained firefighters' gear—helmets, coats, boots, face shields, hoods, gloves. Total outfit: $5,200 per man.

The city of Selma could not buy what we needed. Firefighter company officers at this time were lieutenants and captains. These two ranks were doing the same job.

I said to the mayor and council, "You can save money by doing away with the lieutenant rank and have captains only."

Another goal was completed, in the midst of an election for mayor. Smitherman had been mayor for thirty-five years. He was facing a black man whose name was James Perkins, Jr. Perkins defeated longtime, white Mayor Joe T. Smitherman and became the first black mayor in Selma history.

Selma would supposedly undergo major changes through Selma politics. I knew better and expected that very little would change. All I can say is that you changed horses, but the wagon carried the same baggage.

The new mayor tried to take pages out of Mayor Joe T Smitherman's book and use them. They did not work for him. The new black mayor lacked the ability to use the all-white business structure, which controlled all the revenue and resources in this city and county.

Being the fire chief of the city, I tried to guide the new young, black mayor in how to deal with the white business structure. He failed to listen. He fell on his face very hard. North Selma decided to annex their area and called it Valley Grande, a new city, leaving less revenue for Selma. Our tax base is very low. The new, major battle was never stopped.

Both blacks and whites must work together in order for the city to prosper. We have a new community of all nationalities living here in Selma. What a beautiful flower garden. Who has the wisdom to put this beautiful garden in place? The ground is ready. Who could plant the seeds for economic growth and development in Selma, Alabama?

My next goal as fire chief of the city of Selma was to get the city's fire rating from a class 5 rating to a class 4 rating. I made contact with a consultant from the Fire Services to give me a price on coming to the Selma Fire Department and looking at the Selma water system. The consultant came to Selma, made an assessment on what type of equipment we needed to improve our fire alarm system and brought our training up to date.

My greatest concern was our fire hydrants. They were old and needed to be replaced. The consultant said to me, "It will cost you $1500 for my work." The city council agreed to pay the $1,500 fee. After we made all the corrections the consultant told us to correct, I called the insurance service officer who regulates cities' insurance ratings. The rater came to Selma, Alabama, and rated the city.

We got the rating grade. Selma made a passing grade. This is history for the city of Selma, a milestone. The mayor and council were very happy. This reduced rate caused insurance rates for homes and businesses to drop. To achieve this goal, the Selma Fire Department was very happy.

It was time for a new election. Mayor James Perkins, Jr. had served two four-year terms. We now have George P. Evans running for mayor, another black man. George P. Evans defeated James Perkins, Jr. for the mayoral job.

I now have worked for four different mayors—two white mayors, two black mayors. If you asked me how different they were, I would say very little. Politics has no gender or race. It is what it is.

After thirty-seven years with fourteen and a half years as fire chief, I am "tired." It is time to retire.

The mayor asked me to help him pass a bond so the city of Selma could use the funds to repair all five firehouses and buy new equipment: one new fire engine and a new rescue truck. The bond would be $12 million. We needed the citizens to vote Yes. The bond passed. What a blessing!

I had set September 30, 2009, for my retirement day celebration. It was held at the Carl Morgan Civic Center. The public was invited. We had over 350 guests. What a time we had. My daughter, Madison, played on her guitar the song "Precious Memories." To the State of Alabama, Dallas County, the Probate Judge, the County Commission, Mayor George P. Evans and the City Council—Thank you.

It was always important to keep cool under fire!

Hard, Demanding and Dangerous Work Was Performed Daily By All The Men And Women Wearing The Uniform Of Our First Responders
This Was A 'C' Team

Hard, Demanding and Dangerous Work Was Performed Daily By All The Men And Women Wearing The Uniform Of Our First Responders. This Was A 'C' Team.

Fire Chief Henry E. Allen

**We Had Raised All Standards And Had A
Fully Integrated Firefighters Force Since 1972
This Was One Of The 'A' Teams**

We Had Raised All Standards And Has A Fully Integrated Firefighters Force Since 1972. This Was One Of The 'A' Teams

**The Dedicated Members of Selma Fire / Rescue Brought
Real Security To The Lives Of All Selma Citizens
This was a 'B' Team**

The Dedicated Members of Selma Fire / Rescue Brought Real Security To The Lives Of All Selma Citizens
This was a 'B' Team

VII

Activities in "Retirement"

I was called to service after my retirement. My work has not slowed down. I volunteer my services to Sophia P. Kingston Elementary School.

Historian Alston Fitts and Fire Chief Henry E. Allen are responsible for the name change from East End School to Sophia P. Kingston.

Ms. Sophia P. Kingston, a black freed slave, founded East End. She had the school built and taught 145 students. At that time East Selma had no school.

Ms. Kingston lived on Pettus Street next to Old Live Oak Cemetery. She walked seven days per week to East Selma to teach students.

My aunt was one of her students. Five days per week teaching, missionary work on Saturday and Sunday. I am still P.T.O. President of Kingston Elementary School.

This is the school I first attended. My tenure as P.T.O. president at Kingston Elementary covers over thirty years. All of my children and grandchildren are no longer here at Kingston. I am still here, giving back my service, a role model and teacher to the kids.

I also volunteer two days a week at Selma High School. I served as P. T. O. president at Clark Elementary and School of Discovery—both sixth-grade schools. My ten-year-old daughter attended Cathedral of Christ the King Academy. She is a fifth grader.

I am P.T.O. president at that school. Every Thursday I teach my daughter's class spelling, language, and history. We get to go on field trips together and Chapel services.

My parents were not able to do what I have been doing for my children and others' children. My goal is to touch as many lives as I can. How can this be done? Only by leading, by setting the example. Somebody is always watching you.

We, as parents, cannot for a minute think that our children don't need our help. Children need their parents' guidance now more than ever before. They are crying out. As parents we are not listening. Many of our children are struggling with behavior problems. The schools are facing an uphill battle. The teachers are having a hard time teaching our children. They lack respect and have very little home training.

In order for our children to grow up and be responsible adults, parents first must be willing to change their behavior: stop degrading school administrators and teachers. Parents should not wait until their child gets into trouble or fails. It is a parent's responsibility to be on a regular schedule for parent and teacher meetings once a month.

At the elementary school level, the percentage of parent participation is twenty-five percent. At the sixth grade level it is twenty percent. The middle school level is fifteen percent. High school parents, for some reason, back off from their children. These parents' involvement is ten percent or less.

The ninth grade is a breaking point for our children. Most of our boys and girls drop out in the ninth grade. For that reason alone, I volunteer two days per week, Wednesday and Friday. I spend most of my time dealing with ninth grade students, showing them, pointing out to them, the importance of completing high school. Some are listening.

Many of our children are dealing with drugs, alcohol, early pregnancy, sex, and depression, broken homes, split families. I can honestly write about our children and what they are dealing with. They know that I care about them. Our children want to be loved and cared for. They feel comfort in sharing their concerns and problems with me.

When a ninth grade student shared with me that she had a drinking problem, it touched me very deeply. I asked the student, "What makes you drink?" The student said to me, "I am going through so many family problems. I drink to calm my nerves." I paused for a minute; I did not ask her any more questions, because I already knew the answer.

All this took place in the Student Adjustment Program. In this program (SAP), I spend most of my day counseling ninth and tenth grade students. This program is designed to help students to get back on the right track. The students' stay in SAP consists of going around the school campus picking up trash and any other details that need to be done. The rules are no talking, no eating, no sleeping, no gum, no cell phone, no pants sagging.

Every time you violate any of the rules while you are in the Student Adjustment Program, more days are added to your time. Classroom teachers can have a student sent to SAP for a number of school and classroom violations, including students being disobedient, fighting, skipping classes, using cell phones, smoking, being tardy, or being out of uniform.

There has never been a dull moment in my life for the past thirty years. In addition to working with children, I am now looking back to the year of 1978. My son was in kindergarten in Clark Elementary School. I was a lieutenant in the Selma Fire and Rescue Department, and Parent and Teacher Association president. I was asked to be Santa Claus for all the kids at Clark school. We brought two red fire engines to school—the start of my servant duties and volunteering.

We were already doing fire prevention for all the kids that lived in the city of Selma and Dallas County. We served a total of seven thousand students, not including hospital, nursing homes, and businesses.

In the year 1986, I got a call to service at East End school. In the year of 2003, the school's name changed. If everyone gave something back, there would never be any shortages. The real reward is trying to make a difference in someone else's life so they can pass it on to someone else.

The Salvation Army is my favorite, because so many people's needs are being met. My tenure as a volunteer for the Salvation Army dates back to 1974. I am still with this organization. Their motto is

"Doing the most good." I serve on the Board of Directors. I am the Coordinator for the Christmas bell ringing fund raising.

I also work with the Angel Tree Drive. The Angel Tree is a Christmas tree with names of children who are in need of help, so they can enjoy a happy Christmas. Last year in 2010, there were nine hundred names placed on trees in different locations, hoping that caring people would adopt an angel.

Last year in December, one week before Christmas, we still had over four hundred Angels not adopted. I went to one of our local radio stations and pleaded to the surrounding communities for help in adopting Angels. One of the local community radio stations did a live broadcast in front of Walmart. The Salvation Army had a large truck parked in front of the Walmart store. The Salvation Army major and I were there. One man adopted two hundred Angels. At the end of the broadcast all the Angels were adopted. The major and I looked at each other and said, "Thank you, Lord, and bless the people that made this happen."

My volunteer work with the Salvation Army will continue. The needs are so great. Every year needs are not decreasing—they are increasing in numbers.

Food and shelter are also important areas. The Salvation Army serves six of the poorest counties in this country. Their paid staff is only three people. They have to rely on the help of volunteers from this community. The Salvation Army closed its Thrift Store, where donated items were sold to the community to help make up the loss of funds. The community stopped donating items and started selling their own goods in flee markets. The city of Selma has outdoor flea markets and indoor flea markets. Very little donations from the community were given to the Salvation Army.

When a person who is in need can get some relief, people are helped socially and spiritually. Some join the church and turn their lives over to Jesus Christ. They enjoy Sunday school, regular church services, youth programs, and Junior Cadets programs. My greatest joy came last year in 2010. My 10-year-old daughter taught piano and guitar lessons at the Salvation Army Chapel for one whole week. I was with her every day.

For the past thirty years, I have volunteered at the American Red Cross, teaching CPR classes to all walks of life. I also helped recruit for blood drives at the end of August 2011. The Black Belt chapter of the American Red Cross no longer has staff members to conduct CPR and other classes, because the main Headquarters in Birmingham, Alabama, cut staff due to a lack of funds.

Selma and Dallas and the surrounding counties are hurt because of these moves. We have to look to the Montgomery chapter of the American Red Cross, which is fifty miles away. I will continue to teach CPR classes in spite of all that has taken place: no pay, just volunteer.

Because the needs are so great in these very poor surrounding counties, God will provide, making way for these two very important organizations so they can continue to meet the needs of those that require services.

Now to the Selma to Montgomery National Historic Trail, the Selma Interpretive Center and the National Park service—US Department of Interior—and the city of Selma. The Selma Interpretive Center opened its doors in March 2011.

I serve as a volunteer at the Interpretive Center. My job at the center is that of a greeter. I make visitors feel welcome. I am also a tour guide. I give visitors to the Interpretive Center a civil rights history lesson. Visitors also get to view a twenty-minute video on civil rights.

I really enjoy sharing my feelings and hands-on experience of the beginning of the Civil Rights Movement here in historic Selma, Alabama.

The first mass meeting, May 14, 1963, was held at the Tabernacle Baptist Church, Reverend L. L. Anderson, pastor. I attended that meeting. James Forman was guest speaker, head of SNCC—"Snick."

We are the chosen generation that the Almighty God used to open the eyes of the world. The torch started at R. B. Hudson High School in 1963 to July 2, 1964, when President Lyndon B. Johnson signed the Civil Rights Act, including Title II—Injunctive Relief AGAINST DISCRIMINATION IN PLACES OF PUBLIC ACCOMMODATION.

We, the Selma youth, were selected, some downtown in Selma, to stage sit-in demonstrations such as that at Carter's drugstore, which had a soda fountain only for whites, testing the new law using another white popular meeting place called Thirsty Boy.

There were many more places we tried to integrate. We encountered harsh treatment; many students were hit with billy clubs and ax handles. We did not lose focus on our main goal: getting the right to vote. At the end of 1964, we were still carrying that torch. We, the youth, knew that we could not vote.

We kept the pressure on Dallas County Sheriff Jim Clark. We led demonstrations to the Dallas County Courthouse daily. We also carried signs.

He became very angry and frustrated with us. He knew that he could do very little to the youth. He took it out on the 105 teachers who tried to register to vote. Sheriff Clark used his billy club to attack blacks who tried to register to vote.

In January 1965, Dr. Martin Luther King arrived here in Selma, Alabama, to spearhead a large voter drive. We, the torchbearers, were still holding the torch. We, the youth, were still leading the way.

On Bloody Sunday, the youth were on the bridge. One of our youth group leaders was on the front line. We, the youth, carried the torch all the way to Montgomery, to the State Capital.

The youth of Selma—all ages—we never gave up the torch. We, the Selma youth, fought a good fight and completed the mission that God put before us. The battle was not our battle. God got the victory. He used the youth as bodies to carry the mission out. On August 6, 1965, President Lyndon B. Johnson signed the Voters Rights Act, which gave all Americans the right to vote.

We are the chosen generation that God used to open the eyes of the whole wide world.

Selma has not embraced its youth for a job well done. We, the youth, from 1963 to 1965 are responsible for the passage of the Voters Rights Act.

Come forward, Selma, and give us, the youth, our rightful place in history!

Fourth Annual Dr. King Celebration
2010
Freedom Award
To Chief Henry Allen

Daughter Madison Plays
At Retirement Party

First Aid Class

Participating in the Jerry Lewis Telethon

Author (center) on Deployment in 1990

My Classmates in the
Executive Fire Officers Course

Recognition Award From Mayor Evans

I always fought hard to

obtain modern equipment

Fourth Annual Dr. King Celebration

Freedom Award To Chief Henry Allen

Reading Dr. Seuss For The Kids

Closure

I acknowledge my Lord and Savior Jesus Christ, who gave me the wisdom and knowledge to write this book.

My life took on real meaning at the age of nine years old. I found myself looking for a job. If you lived in poverty, not knowing where your next meal was coming from, you needed help.

I was given a job by white store owners. This job gave me hope while still living in poverty: never give up.

As I grew older, my eyes began to open up, and my ears would hear things that made my mind say, “Something is missing.”

Now in the eleventh grade, my white coworker and I were studying homework on the job. He looked at my textbook and said to me, “The book you are studying, I studied that book in the ninth grade.” We looked at each other and said, “Something is wrong.”

In the same year as the Civil Rights Movement began, in 1963, I began to really understand what was missing.

Blacks were not allowed the same rights that whites enjoyed. We were second-class citizens. My eyes came wide open, and my ears tuned in.

Two of my classmates started talking about the right to vote, and a man name Bernard Lafayette and ‘Snick.’

I had no idea what they were talking about. They invited me to Tabernacle Baptist Church, the meeting held in the basement. I sat and listened to Lafayette speak and accepted the challenge.

We are the chosen generation that was chosen by the Almighty God to change the course of history.

The torch that was lit in 1963 lead us 54 miles to the State Capital in Montgomery, Alabama, in 1965, and the same year on August 7, President Lyndon B. Johnson signed the Voters Rights Act.

I say to all the families that lost loved ones, their labor was not in vain. People from all walks of life made sure that the torch would not go out. I thank all of you. May God bless you.